BOYS OF STEEL

ALFRED A. KNOPF

NEW YORK

The CREATORS OF SUPERMAN

BY
MARC TYLER NOBLEMAN

ILLUSTRATED BY
ROSS MacDONALD

Most days, Jerry Siegel slipped into the halls of his high school staring at the floor. He always wished he were going in the other direction—back home.

That's where he could be with his friends. They were an extraordinary bunch.

But Tarzan, Flash Gordon, and Buck Rogers were fictional characters. They saved other fictional characters in pulp magazines and comic strips. They couldn't save anyone in the real world, where millions of people were struggling to find jobs during the Great Depression of the 1930s. They couldn't save Jerry's father, who had died of heart failure during an after-hours robbery in his clothing store in Cleveland.

Jerry read amazing stories every evening, every weekend, every chance he got. If he wasn't reading, he was watching—the cinemas had no shortage of rousing motion pictures about daredevils who laughed at danger. And when he should have been paying attention in class, he let his thoughts drift to galaxies yet to be explored. None of it helped him miss his father less, but it did distract him from his sadness for a little while.

Jerry also wrote his own adventure and science fiction stories. He'd pound away at his typewriter by the front window in his attic. From there, he could see boys playing ball and flirting with girls on the street below. Jerry wasn't good at those things. He had crushes on girls who didn't know—or didn't care—that he existed. "Some of them look like they *hope* I don't exist," Jerry thought.

Jerry was shy—unless he could talk about musclemen or detectives or jet packs or ray guns or any other champions or gadgets he'd read about. But the kids he knew weren't interested in those weird tales, and they ignored Jerry.

Except Joe Shuster.

Jerry and Joe could've passed for brothers. Both were short. Both wore glasses. Like Jerry, Joe was lousy at sports and mousy around girls. He, too, was shy, almost painfully so. And he, too, escaped to other worlds in pulps and strips, then made up his own worlds.

But he did it with pictures, not words. While Jerry was typing in his attic, Joe was drawing in his kitchen, using a breadboard as a surface. Joe often illustrated Jerry's stories.

No matter the obstacle, Joe found a way to draw. When his family couldn't afford art paper, he made do with wrapping paper from the butcher or the back of discarded wallpaper. In winter, because the Shusters' apartment had no heat, he drew while bundled in several sweaters, one or two coats—even gloves.

It wasn't just kids who didn't understand Jerry and Joe. One of Jerry's teachers told him that he was wasting his time writing what she called "trash." But Jerry sensed that these stories were important. In life, people got pushed around. Children lost parents. Criminals got away. In stories, heroes could prevent all of that.

And Jerry had a plan. If he and Joe could come up with a colorful new character, they could produce a comic strip about him—and maybe sell it to a newspaper syndicate.

The partners crafted "a science fiction story in cartoons." It starred a brave, tough man who fought for truth and justice. But that wasn't enough to make him stand out from the many other men of action already on the newsstands. After only one publisher said no to Jerry and Joe's concept, Joe tore up the pages in disappointment.

Late one summer night in 1934, Jerry couldn't sleep. The air sagged from the heat, but that was not why Jerry was still awake.

"What if I was real terrific?" Jerry thought. "What if I had something special going for me, like jumping over buildings or throwing cars around? Then maybe people would notice me."

Jerry knew he would never be able to do anything like that—
but suddenly he was struck with the idea of a hero who could. He hopped
up to scribble it down. After he flopped back into bed, more vivid details
about this hero began flickering in his brain. Two hours later, he sprang up
again, stumbled, and wrote those ideas down.

This went on all night.

The character would be like Samson, Hercules, and all the strongmen Jerry had ever heard of, rolled into one. "Only more so," Jerry thought.

But he would not be a man in the jungle, in space, or in the future. Actually, he would not be a man at all. This hero would be an alien.

Not a slimy green giant with two hundred eyes who prowled a distant moon and snacked on astronauts.

Rather, an alien who protected humans. An alien who even looked human. An alien who came from far away and now lived on Earth. The real Earth, the Great Depression Earth.

That was something different. The other heroes Jerry and Joe read about were regular humans in strange places. This hero would be a stranger in a regular place.

He would have impenetrable skin, phenomenal speed, and tremendous agility—like, say, a habit of leaping so high that it would look as though he were flying. Joe would like that.

The hero would have the confidence to speak to any woman. Joe would <u>really</u> like that.

But even heroes need a break, so this one would have a secret identity.

"Then he would be meek and mild, like Joe and I are, and wear glasses, like we do," Jerry thought. No one would guess that such a hero was also someone like *them*.

Before dawn, Jerry tugged on his clothes over his pajamas. He dashed out without eating. Jerry didn't run much. But that morning he ran faster than a speeding bullet, nine and a half blocks to Joe's apartment.

In breathless spurts, Jerry described to Joe what he'd imagined. When he was done, Jerry pushed his glasses back up his nose. He ripped out a sheet from his notebook and handed it to Joe, who grabbed a pencil.

Joe leaned close to the paper, as he usually did. Jerry leaned over Joe's shoulder, as he usually did. Even with his glasses on, Joe squinted. He began to sketch. His vision was blurry but his art wasn't. In seconds, the hero in Jerry's mind was coming to life on Joe's page.

Just as Jerry had written all night, Joe kept drawing all day. His eyes grew tired before his hand, but he was too excited to stop. Jerry had known this hero would be strong, but it was not until he gazed at Joe's designs that he realized how strong.

He would be as strong as steel.

And because they had created him, Jerry and Joe felt as strong as steel, too.

Their hero was more than good, even more than great. They studied his costume. "Let's put something on the front," Joe said.

They decided on an "S."
For "super."
"And for 'Siegel' and 'Shuster,'" Jerry said.

The boys thought this hero might be their big idea. They prepared
a series of comic strips about him and again set out to find a publisher.
For more than three years, editors turned them down. Finally, one
said yes.

His company was putting out a new type of magazine called a
comic book. He asked Jerry and Joe if they would rearrange their
comic strips to fit that format. They happily agreed.

One of the owners took one look at Joe's cover drawing and shook his head. "Nobody's going to believe this," he said.

But Jerry and Joe believed it, just as they believed Tarzan could yak with apes and Flash Gordon could move to another planet and Buck Rogers could wake from a coma after five hundred years.

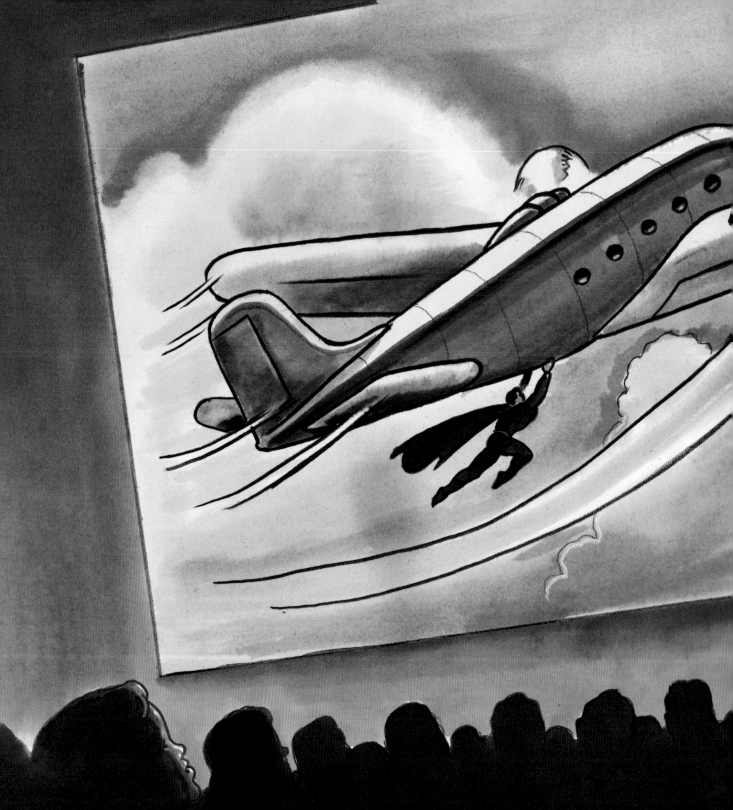

The Great Depression had lasted nearly a decade. Now a world war was brewing. Everyday people were about to be called to duty, and many would prove to be real-life heroes. But if there was ever a time for a fantasy hero, particularly one with powers and abilities far beyond those of mortal men, it was then. People wanted a hero they knew would always come home. Jerry and Joe gave them that—the world's first superhero.

He debuted in 1938. His comic book was an instant hit. Soon he also won fans in a comic strip, on the radio, in animated shorts, in books, and in movie serials. When television caught on, he got a show there, too. He continued to soar up, up, and away.

Some people look up in the sky and see a bird or a plane, but nothing beyond. In the trying days of yesteryear, Jerry and Joe looked up and saw a star no one had discovered before. They brought him to Earth and watched him become a superstar.

And today, on every story where
his name appears, theirs do, too.

The Greatest Superhero of All Time

Superman went on to rescue just about everybody from just about anything. No cat stuck in a tree was insignificant, no menace threatening the universe was insurmountable. Two people he couldn't save in the nick of time, however, were his creators.

Both Jerry and Joe were born in 1914. They met in high school in 1930 and created Superman just after graduation. They turned twenty-four the year he rocketed from Krypton directly into pop culture immortality with the first issue of *Action Comics*.

Worried they might not have another chance to get Superman published, these young men had sold that first Superman story—and all rights to the character—to the company that is now DC Comics, publisher of *Action Comics*, for $130.

In those early years of the comic book industry, there were writers and artists who did retain ownership of their creations, but the majority saw little reason to. For every Superman, there were hundreds of do-gooders such as Enchanted Dagger and Micro-Face who sold poorly and vanished from the magazine racks faster than a—well, you know.

With a startling cover image of Superman lifting a car over his head, *Action* #1 had a first print run of 200,000. (It cost ten cents. Fewer than a hundred copies are known to exist today, and the ones in the best condition are worth more than $500,000.) *Action* featured several heroes, but kids began to clamor for "that magazine with Superman in it." In 1939, Superman became the first character created for comic books to get his own series. Combined, *Action* and *Superman* were selling more than a million copies a month. The Superman newspaper strip also debuted in 1939—and soon had a circulation of 20 million.

In 1940, a popular magazine named *Look* ran a two-page strip by Jerry and Joe imagining how Superman could end World War II. In a mere few panels, he captures Adolf Hitler and Joseph Stalin and delivers them for judgment before world leaders. A recurring claim that Hitler himself banned Superman comics because he interpreted Superman as a Jew is almost certainly untrue, though a major Nazi newspaper did mock Jerry's Jewishness two months after the *Look* piece. (Somehow Joe, who was also Jewish, escaped insult.) Jerry and Joe did not specify a religion for Superman, but his Kryptonian name is Kal-El, which in Hebrew can mean "all that is God" or "all that God is."

Though Jerry and Joe did not get a fixed percentage of Superman dollars, they commanded sizable salaries as DC employees. When they asked for a cut of Superman profits, DC said they should be happy with what they had. This intensified Jerry and Joe's growing resentment toward their publisher.

During World War II, Jerry served in the army, while Joe was exempt from military service because of his failing eyesight. After the war, Jerry in particular was no longer willing to settle for a minimal share of the success of Superman. In 1947, he and Joe sued DC for $5 million and the rights to Superman. They lost but were offered $100,000 if they would surrender all claims to their brainchild. Knowing an appeal would be too expensive, they accepted—then were promptly fired. On top of that, their names were removed from Superman comics.

Jerry had written almost every Superman story until he'd been drafted in 1943. Joe had inked every Superman face for nearly ten years, even after the workload had become so taxing that he needed a team of artists to help with the rest. But a decade after Superman launched himself and the superhero comic book industry to boot, Jerry and Joe found themselves cut off from their greatest achievement. They felt DC had stolen their Man of Steel.

In 1948, Jerry married Joanne Carter, whom he'd met when she posed for Joe around 1936—the first live model for Superman's sweetheart, Lois Lane. In the 1950s, Jerry wrote comics when he could, often struggling to find assignments. In 1959, DC decided to give him work again, but he was not credited and could not publicly state that he was the co-creator of Superman. Fans feel that his stories of that period were some of his finest. In 1966, he challenged DC's renewal of the Superman copyright. For the second time, Jerry lost both his job at DC and his case. He became a mail clerk for $7,000 a year.

Nearing blindness, Joe settled into a life of solitude, but hardly in a fortress. He and his younger brother Frank moved to an apartment in Queens, New York. While Frank worked to support them both, Joe kept to himself.

In 1975, news broke that Warner Bros. Studios had paid DC $3 million for the rights to make a star-studded Superman movie. Marlon Brando, cast as Superman's Kryptonian father, Jor-El, would earn $3.7 million—for a role requiring only twelve days of shooting. Jerry and Joe, then in their sixties, would pocket nothing.

Upon reading about *Superman: The Movie*, Jerry found that he still had some of the crusader in him—only this time, he went not to the courts but to the press. He crafted a nine-page diatribe accusing DC of ruining his and Joe's lives by getting rich off their creation while allowing them both to descend to the edge of poverty. He asked the public to boycott all Superman merchandise and shame DC into compensating them. Then he bombarded a thousand news organizations with the Superman story DC never wanted to tell.

The media began to cover the situation. Several high-profile artists on good terms with DC took up the cause, too. Jay Emmett, the executive vice president of Warner Communications, which was the parent company of DC, said, "Legally, nothing has to be done. Morally, I think something should be done, and we will do it out of compassion."

Warner announced that it would provide Jerry and Joe with $20,000 annually (an amount that would increase over time), medical insurance, and continuing support for their families in case of their deaths. DC also agreed to restore their names to their creation. All Superman stories in all media—including the film—would bear the words "Superman created by Jerry Siegel and Joe Shuster." This was the quieter part of the deal, but it meant more to Jerry and Joe than can be calculated.

Neither lived to see another major victory. In March 2008, a judge awarded Jerry's widow and daughter half of the U.S. copyright to the material in Action Comics #1. This may entitle them to up to 50 percent of U.S. profits from Superman since 1999. Joe's family has also entered the arena to assert its right to the other half, meaning that DC could be legally obligated to transfer all U.S. rights to Superman to the families of his creators. Negotiations are ongoing.

Joe died a bachelor in 1992. DC devoted a page in its comics to his passing. Joe's name and life span were written in black within a solid white Superman shield. Jerry was quoted underneath: "The comic book field has lost a great artist and a true pioneer."

Four years later, Jerry died, leaving Joanne, a son, a daughter, and two grandsons. DC again ran a full-page commemoration. Over a gray-tone Superman symbol and above Jerry's birth and death years, a four-line epitaph honored the man who "taught us to fly."

In 1936, Jerry and Joe had scribbled down phrases to pitch Superman to publishers. These included "the strip destined to sweep the nation," "the greatest single event since the birth of comic strips," and the title of this afterword— "the greatest superhero of all time." They were charmingly bold boasts that came true—and still are true more than seventy years later.

Marc Tyler Nobleman
July 2008

To Daniela and Lara, my Girls of Steel
—M.T.N.

To my parents, the first superheroes
I ever knew—R.McD.

ACKNOWLEDGMENTS

Many generously contributed time and knowledge to
this book, a few of whom I have space to thank again:
Dennis Dooley, Brad Ricca, Gerard Jones, Dwight
Decker, Mike Sangiacomo, Dan Musson at the
Cleveland City Planning Commission, Ann Sindelar
and Sean Martin at the Western Reserve Historical
Society, Marian Wallace at Glenville High School, the
Gray family, Phil Yeh, John Sherwood, Jeff Trexler,
Jennifer Wingertzahn, Jill Phillips, Laurie Stempler,
Ross MacDonald, my mom and dad, and especially
Janet Schulman.

SELECTED SOURCES

Andrae, Thomas. "Of Supermen and Kids with
    Dreams," an interview with Jerry Siegel, Joe
    Shuster, and Joanne Siegel. *The Official Overstreet
    Comic Book Price Guide 1988–1989.* 18th ed.
    New York: The House of Collectibles, 1988.
Daniels, Les. *Superman: The Complete History.* San
    Francisco: Chronicle Books, 1998.
Dooley, Dennis. "The Man of Tomorrow and the Boys
    of Yesterday." *Superman at Fifty: The Persistence of
    a Legend.* Cleveland: Octavia Press, 1987.
Jones, Gerard. *Men of Tomorrow: Geeks, Gangsters, and
    the Birth of the Comic Book.* New York: Basic
    Books, 2004.

All dialogue is excerpted from interviews with Jerry and Joe.

THIS IS A BORZOI BOOK PUBLISHED BY ALFRED A. KNOPF

Text copyright © 2008 by Marc Tyler Nobleman
Illustrations copyright © 2008 by Ross MacDonald
Hand lettering by David Coulson

All rights reserved. Published in the United States by Alfred A.
Knopf, an imprint of Random House Children's Books, a division
of Random House, Inc., New York.

Knopf, Borzoi Books, and the colophon are registered trademarks
of Random House, Inc.

Visit us on the Web! www.randomhouse.com/kids

Educators and librarians, for a variety of teaching tools, visit us at
www.randomhouse.com/teachers

Library of Congress Cataloging-in-Publication Data
Nobleman, Marc Tyler.
Boys of steel : the creators of Superman / by Marc Tyler Nobleman ;
illustrated by Ross MacDonald. — 1st ed.
    p.   cm.
ISBN 978-0-375-83802-6 (trade) —
ISBN 978-0-375-93802-3 (lib. bdg.)
1. Siegel, Jerry, 1914–1996—Juvenile literature.
2. Shuster, Joe—Juvenile literature.
3. Cartoonists—United States—Biography—Juvenile literature.
I. MacDonald, Ross. II. Title.
NC1305.N63 2008
741.5092'2—dc22
2007041606

The text of this book is set in 15-point Goudy.

MANUFACTURED IN CHINA

August 2008

10 9 8 7 6 5 4 3 2 1

First Edition